Messed Up

Jim Kitty

Copyright

Table of Contents

Introduction

Are you aware that many local and state police departments don't have the highest regard for our federal law enforcement agencies? For example, some call the FBI the "Federal Bureau of Idiots".

Why is this, especially when the news media tends to glorify federal law enforcement agencies? How many times have we heard a news reporter say "the investigation is now being led by the FBI"? As though this is a good thing and that we can now rest easy!

The truth is that there are significant areas of dysfunction and waste that exists within our federal law enforcement agencies. Unfortunately, dysfunction in our essential enforcement agencies can literally be lethal for the general public. This book is intended to make everyone aware of these issues; but more importantly, the book is a call to action for all concerned citizens. These issues can be resolved with your help.

Currently, there are 15 primary federal law enforcement agencies that are tasked with protecting the citizens of our great country. They share a common goal, get the bad guy before they do us harm. But why are there so many agencies, do we really need this many? The reality is that the sheer number of agencies is actually one of the biggest problems. You know what they say about having too many cooks in the kitchen.

It's estimated that there are more than 500,000 government employees working for our federal law enforcement agencies. And as discussed in this book, there is likely three times that number of federal contractors working for these agencies. This brings the total number of people working for these agencies to approximately 2 million.

The total combined annual budgets are not readily publicized; although, it very likely exceeds two trillion dollars.

Keep in mind that the federal government is notorious for over spending and messing things up. They have a track record that speaks for itself. It's one thing to misuse our tax dollars but it's a much more serious matter when it comes to protecting the general public from terrorist and low-life criminals.

It would have been wonderful if federal law enforcement agencies had intercepted the

9/11 terrorist before they boarded those planes and inflected so much terror on the entire country. Additionally, it would have been wonderful if the Boston terrorists or the ISIS inspired Orlando terrorist had been arrested beforehand.

Since 9/11 there have been far too many acts of terror perpetrated against U.S. citizens. For a complete list of all terror acts that have occurred in this country since 9/11, refer to the last chapter of this book where I have documented the 16 most recent acts of terror.

We owe it to ourselves to make sure that our federal law enforcement agencies are the best that they can be and that they are always one step ahead of the next act of senseless terror.

Unfortunately, we are not where we should be and we must act quickly to become much more effective.

There are a number of very specific items that we can do to ensure that our government addresses these problems as quickly as possible. Let's join together in this much needed effort.

I believe in the keep-it-simple approach to everything in life and maintain this mantra in this book. You should find this book to be an easy-read and you will discover motivation to join others in making America a better and stronger nation by fixing the many issues that currently exist within our federal law enforcement agencies.

Great Expectations

We have very high expectations of law enforcement in general and we know that our federal law enforcement agencies are extremely important in protecting us from the worst of the worst. We do realize that they have a very difficult job and we want and expect these agencies to work flawlessly.

Our exceptions is that our law enforcement agencies strive for a perfect record in stopping every terrorist and every low-life criminal BEFORE they are able to execute any barbaric acts of terror.

Examples of our expectations:

We expect that they will work tirelessly in protecting all citizens but most importantly that they put an end to crimes that impact our innocent children and our senior citizens.

We expect that no Islamic terrorist will ever again inflict their sub-human horror upon our citizens.

We expect that the volume and flow of illegal drugs into our country be reduced every year from this point forward.

We expect that they will find a solution for and put an end to all cybercrimes as soon as possible.

We expect that they continually police their forces to ensure that they treat all citizens in a fair and just manner during any enforcement activity.

We expect that our borders are protected from illegals crossing into the country. And when they do, that they are quickly captured and sent back to their country of origin.

We expect that they will make sure that our elected officials always act in the best interest of their electorates and when they fail to do this that they are prosecuted to the fullest extent of the law.

We expect that they will make sure that all local and state police departments always act in the best interest of the general public.

We expect that they will prosecute any government official to the fullest extent possible that is convicted of public corruption at any government level.

We expect that every tax dollar entrusted with these agencies is used to its fullest benefit and not spent in a reckless fashion.

In order to meet our high expectations it is extremely important that we demand the best from our federal law enforcement agencies. In many areas we are not where we need to be at this time. Many tax payer dollars are being wasted in the process.

We are well aware that federal government has a reputation for not been very good when it comes to spending our tax dollars wisely, and in many well documented cases they have wasted many millions of dollars in many different areas. As we will see throughout this book there are many areas where we need to make significant changes to ensure that this no longer happens.

We must look back at our past and understand why we have made mistakes and hopefully learn from this so that we can have a better future.

At this time in our history it is extremely important that we begin to do a better job, especially in the area of federal law enforcement. We must begin to use our resources in the most judicious manner possible.

We need to do all that we can do to make sure that every tax dollar spent is spent wisely.

I have written this book with the expectation and hope that we can start afresh with a new federal law enforcement agency that will make all Americans safer and more secure in our daily lives.

Toxic Times

Our nation has endured many periods of extreme terror. The Civil War comes to mind when we were torn apart from within and so many brave North and South soldiers lost their lives. World War II was a time of great conflict and terror for our nation. The Vietnam War and many other conflicts were also trying and tragic events in our history.

Today we face a new type of terror, one that may be more barbaric than any other that we have seen before.

And with today's modern age of technology the weapons of terror are not just bullets and bombs. Computers and software are now used as weapons of terror. Computers of all sizes can be used against us, from handheld smart phones to the largest computers that run our factories, our hospitals and our utilities.

Islamic terror organizations such as ISIS and Al Qaeda use everyday software programs and apps to plan and execute their brutal terror attacks. They also use these software tools to recruit others to act on their behalf to inflict terror.

We all realize that Islamic terrorists are more ruthless than any other enemy that we have ever encounter before. Their sole mission in life is to end ours. They believe this is the directive of their god and will be rewarded in the next life for completing their mission.

We must realize that the ideology of Islamic terror groups is what it is and will never change.

In addition to Islamic terror, we have other criminals that present a massive challenge for law enforcement. Cyber-attacks from foreign governments are constantly attempting to cause massive problems for our nation.

The government of North Korea has thousands of computer hackers dedicated to inflecting major computer outages within the United States. Unfortunately, North Korea is not alone, as there are other countries that are also intent on inflecting harm on the United States.

Lower level criminals also use cyber weapons to infect our computer systems for financial gain. They are able to collect untraceable ransoms using financial networks such as Bitcoin. Bonny and Clyde are probably wishing that they lived during these times instead of in the 1930's.

The Bonny and Clyde's of today don't carry six-shooters. They also don't need to hide in remote boarding houses, they can easily hide behind their computer screens from anywhere in the world. In 1930 we only had one set of Bonny and Clyde' to deal with, today we have countless thousands.

In many cases these criminals live abroad in other countries and use the internet to reach out and commit their criminal acts remotely. They have no fear of any consequences since their governments will not assist the U.S. in bringing them to justice.

This truly is very toxic times and we all must be on our "A" game at all times to be ahead of the evil that is always one step behind us and sometimes one step ahead of us. We are not nearly as prepared as we need to be to combat this level of terror.

This is why we really need to make sure that our federal law enforcement agencies are as good as they can be in every sense of the word.

We must get very serious, very quickly to combat this ever growing enemy.

Social Media

To think the term social media didn't even exist a few short years ago. And now using our handheld computer smartphones everyone can communicate so simply. This is a wonderful thing; that is for law abiding citizens.

Those that want to do us harm, quickly figured out how to use Facebook, Twitter and other social media tools for their benefit. These evil-doers use all forms of social media to recruit others, to terrorize others and to communicate with their partners in crime.

They quickly determined that the companies that developed these social media software apps where more concerned with market share and making a profit than they were about ensuring that their products were not used for nefarious reasons.

Some software companies have intentionally designed their apps with a focus on anonymity; giving any criminal complete confidence of never being identified. Within such apps, criminals can freely exchange child pornography or terror planning without any fear of being identified and arrested.

People are now able to communicate with large groups of people with great ease very quickly.

Let's take a quick trip backwards, about 40 years ago. Prior to 1970, the media consisted mainly of broadcast TV, radio stations and the newspaper. All of which was one-way communications and it was actually controlled by the Federal Communications Commission (FCC).

In those days, social media simply did not exist. The closest thing to social media back then took place on the street corner, at a local bar or in small gatherings. A far cry from what we have today.

In the 1970's, cable TV started to become widely used and the introduction of the internet occurred in the early 1990's. The combination of these two industries have forever shaped our lives and culture in many ways.

Prior to the introduction of these new industries, the general public really had no way to effectively communicate with the masses. The closest thing to it was hard copy print via books and newspapers, both of which can't compete with the quickness and impact that can be achieved in today's social media world.

Another reality was that prior to the 1970's, the FCC ruled the airways with an iron-fist. They prohibited broadcast TV and radio stations from airing any content that was considered objectionable in any manner.

The FCC prohibited "obscene and indecent" material.

Programming was considered obscene if "the average person, would find the material to be obscene." They defined indecent programming as "patently offensive as measured by contemporary community standards for the broadcast medium if it described sexual activities or sexual organs."

The FCC had the power to restrict content and to censor obscene material. They also required a balance and "fairness" in political programming and required that a certain percentage of each broadcast week be devoted to what was called "public use."

During that period in our history when the FCC controlled the airways, there was simply no way for a private citizen or for that matter even a TV journalist to communicate anything that was considered objectionable material.

Fast forward to today and so much has changed. So much of our political discourse and rhetoric is harmful and unfortunately this has become the norm.

Objectionable material drives ratings and that appears to be the only barometer that broadcast companies use these days.

The FCC apparently has lost all of its ability to control content.

Political discourse has become more and more toxic in recent years. America has a clear separation between two large groups of people. We call them far-right and far-left groups. Yes, there are still people in a third group that fall somewhere in the middle.

Although, it's the far-right and far-left people that are extremely outspoken and at times go way overboard in expressing or supporting their views. In some cases these people turn to violence and literally wish for evil consequences for anyone that does not share their views.

Far-right and far-left people have always existed; the problem is that in today's agile social media environment, these people can very easily reach thousands or with the assistance of cable and broadcast TV even millions of people in less time than it takes to eat dinner.

We need to understand this brutal reality. Social media in its current state are wonderful convenience tools for law abiding citizens to freely communicate and socialize. Although we also need to realize that these same tools become valuable weapons that are exploited by mean people and far worse by terrorist and criminals.

The big question for us as a society is where do we go from here as it relates to social media content?

Should we consider a return to our past or should we continue to stay the course and allow for a completely open and free social media environment?

Dysfunctional Agencies

As noted in the introduction, I will put forth a strong recommendation that most of our current federal law enforcement agencies need to be combined or merged into a single federal agency. But first, it's important to understand just how dysfunctional these agencies have become over time.

Understand that the primary goal of merging these agencies is to vastly improve their collective abilities to disable criminals and terrorist before they are able to inflict harm on our citizens. While this is the primary goal, the beneficial side effect will be a massive cost savings each and every year.

Let's look at just a few areas of dysfunction:

Data Sharing

The primary goal of each agency is to catch bad guys and protect the American public. As you can imagine, there are many databases where bad-guy profiles, investigations and histories are stored.

The problem is that each agency has its own unique databases. Sometimes there are processes and procedures in place that are designed to share bad-guy data between agencies. These sharing processes take time and are prone to failure for one reason or another.

Delayed sharing or failure of sharing a single data-point for a single bad-guy can be the difference between intercepting a bad-guy before an event as opposed to showing up after a tragic event has occurred.

A simple analogy to this problem is that we don't have separate checking accounts for each type of bill that we have, because if we did that, you can be sure that you will be late transferring the necessary funds from one account to another in a timely manner to pay an important bill. You would end up with many NSF fees every year.

As it is now, there are simply too many databases spread across too many agencies. It's just common sense that this would create issues and problems.

Law Enforcement Training

Every federal law enforcement agency has at its core thousands of law enforcement officers. For example, there are FBI Agents, DHS Agents and ATF Agents, etc.

Each agency has its own training facilities and curriculums that cost the tax payers millions of dollars every year. While the training objectives are very much the same for each agency, each agency has its own unique approach and curriculum. Basically reinventing the wheel at each agency.

Providing the level of training needed for these agents is one of the most expensive components within each agency. New agents spend more than 3-months of intensive and dedicated training. Additionally, agents continue to receive many weeks of ongoing training every year for their entire career.

Having more than a dozen different agencies needing to conduct such training is simply illogical. Imagine the duplication of so many resources. The tax dollars that could be saved by having these agencies combine their training facilities and resources would be in the billions of dollars.

A valid comparison would be to look at the training that the U.S. Army provides.

Every year many more young men and women join the Army than those that join a Federal Law Enforcement agency. The Army does this using a shared training curriculum. This offers economies of scale and ensures that every Army recruit receives the same training.

Due to the sheer volume, the U.S. Army does have multiple sites for training: Fort Jackson, Fort Sill, Fort Leonard, Fort Knox and Fort Benning. Although they share the same training curriculum and training resources.

Computers and Software

Everything is computerized and this is surly the case within every government agency. There are software applications that have specific law enforcement processes. Many software applications cost these agencies millions and even billions of dollars every year.

Most software is developed by outside companies and are also maintained by outside companies. For example, let's look at a very simple software application that is needed by every federal law enforcement agency.

Let's call this application "agent assets". This application is needed to allow each agent to keep track of all government assets assigned to them. For example, their fire arms, ammunition, bullet proof vests and their badge. Agents can very easily have more than 200 assets under their control at anytime. These assets must be accurately tracked and accounted for at all times and returned to inventory when the agent retires or leaves the agency.

Custom software applications need to be developed and maintained for "agent assets", which is understandable. Although, what is not acceptable is having a dozen or more of the same software applications developed and supported when we could and should need only one "agent assets" application.

If the federal government could answer this question "how much do we spend on computers and software every year to support more than a dozen key law enforcement agencies?" Well, there are so many components they simply don't know and would be ashamed to share this number with the general public. Carl Sagan (famous astrophysicist) used to refer to the cosmos by saying "billions and billions". You can be sure that is certainly the case if you were able to identify all computer and software expenditures made every year by these agencies.

Software and computer companies are the only beneficiaries from the dysfunction of these agencies as it relates to technology.

Government Vehicles

You may be surprised to learn that every federal law enforcement agent has their own government car funded by the tax payers. These cars are to be used for official government use only. Although all federal agents use their government cars when they commute to and from work.

All federal agents are assigned to a specific office location; this could be at headquarters in D.C. or at one of the hundreds of federal offices throughout the country. These agents obviously need to travel to and from their home every day to their assigned office. They drive from their home to work everyday in in their assigned government cars. Commuting to and from work is considered official business travel; so, they are permitted to do this.

The reality is that most agents use their government vehicle to do ONLY this. Most agents spend their entire day at the office as opposed to being on the road conducting some arrest or for some other official business activity.

The bottom line is that 90 percent or more of the total miles accumulated on all federal agents cars are those miles used to commute to and from their homes.

So, why is it that federal agents can't use their personal vehicle to compute to and from work like everyone else in the world? The answer is simply that they should and the tax payers should not be footing the bill for their travel expenses to and from work.

There are obviously times when agents need to use their cars for actual official business, i.e. for arrests or for court appearances. These needs can be accommodated for by simply having a pool of federal cars at each federal office that can freely be used by agents whenever business travel is necessary.

State police and city police departments have always used a shared pooled vehicle concept. Each officer does not have their own personal squad car. They drive to their assigned station in their personal vehicle and then are assigned a squad car for their days shift. If this concept works for local police departments there is no reason why it can't work for federal agents.

So, the net effect is that a federal office where 100 agents are based, instead of having 100 government cars in the parking lot, the office could have a pool of 20 or 25 cars on-the-ready at all times.

The feds would likely save more than 2 billion dollars every year if they were to begin to use a shared vehicle pool concept.

This is just another example of where the federal government does not spend our tax dollars in a judicious fashion.

Admin Departments

Any large organization needs to have many support and admin departments in order to function properly. A large public corporation has many departments and divisions. The same is true for government agencies; although, they have even more divisions due to their congressional oversight and congressional interface requirements.

Just as in private industry, our government agencies have all of the standard departments. For example, accounting, payroll, human resources and legal departments just to name a few.

Unfortunately, when it comes to the federal law enforcement we have more than a dozen of every one of these departments. All doing very similar work at the tax payers' expense.

You can be certain that there are dozens and dozens of other agencies that should or could be merged or completely eliminated. It has been said that no one actually knows how many government agencies exist; since there are so many that the general public never hears about. That being said, I will limit the scope of this evaluation to our federal law enforcement agencies.

Top Heavy Management

Government agencies are notorious for having far too many supervisors and management levels. At times, there are more managers than people in the trenches actually doing real productive work.

Having too many levels of management is actually more of a problem than first imagined. When there are too many levels of management within an organization these managers need to find something to do to keep busy and to stay relevant within the organization.

One of the most popular activities that happens in government is reorganizations. Management decides when it's time to play musical chairs in their division or group. They don't actually need to have evidence that a reorganization will be beneficial; although they always attempt to communicate to their management that it is the right thing to do at the time. Truth be told, it generates some exposure for them and keeps them busy.

The effect of most of these reorganizations is counter-productive. You basically move many people from doing a job that they have become proficient in performing into a job where they are less than proficient.

Another popular activity that management frequently dreams up is department and group name changes. Again, this is another wasteful process that simply generates lots of busy work for people. For example, if a group changes its name from "Process Control Group" to "Design Services" this may sound like that's no big deal. The reality is that almost every department document will need to reflect this change, every web page will need to be changed, business cards, audio and video content. That's just to name a few items that will need to be changed. Since its government dollars and resources that are involved, a cost benefit analysis is never performed to determine if this type of change makes sense. The only thing of value is normally this gives management a sense of moving forward and doing something.

Since there are so many federal law enforcement agencies doing pretty much the same thing the problem of having far too many supervisors and levels of management is significantly amplified.

Shameful Work Ethics

Why is it that private industry workers are so much more productive than government employees? This is absolutely true, and there are many reasons for this.

It's in the water or in the air within every government office. Anyone that comes from private industry and becomes a government employee will feel it and taste it almost immediately.

From day-1 during new employee orientation you discover that there is never a sense of urgency about anything. You discover and feel like you have returned to elementary school. You find yourself watching a bunch of boring orientation videos most of which cover common sense topics that 8th graders know. They do stop short of reminding new employees to wash their hands when using the rest rooms, although they are likely preparing such a video on this topic right now. :)

Once you graduate from elementary school (again) and report to your duty station you need to be prepared for nothing. In most cases they really have nothing for you to do, since they already have more than enough people to perform the assigned work.

While there are exceptions to the scenario just described, unfortunately they are the exceptions.

One of the most important tasks that every government employee must learn immediately is how to fill out you time sheet;

which these days is done online using your assigned desktop computer. Although, beware that getting your login credentials may delay this for many days or even weeks. You will find that this actually seems like the most important task you will do every week until you retire.

A supervisor's most common communications with their group is reminding them to make sure that their time sheets are filed in a timely manner. It's like they earn brownie points with their management when they get their entire department to complete their time sheets ahead of schedule. The reality is that government supervisors don't have a lot to do, so they want to make sure that the few things that they are responsible for is accomplished in a timely manner.

It's hard to fathom that time sheets are the first and most important topic to be addressed. It's true and the truth really hurts and speaks volumes for why productivity is so very low within government agencies.

Let's move on to the second most discussed topic within every government agency "retirement".

Never a day will pass where you don't hear or talk to someone about when they plan to retire or whose retirement party is upcoming. It seems like you're expected to begin planning for your retirement on the second day of your new job. At the very least be prepared to spend several hours every week on the topic of retirement.

In private industry when someone retires, their retirement party is after work hours and is at some local restaurant. This is normally not the case in the government.

Government retirement parties are typically schedule from 11am to 2pm on site in a government conference room. Coworkers generally prepare the food in an effort to keep their cost down. The retirement party planning, preparation and cleanup is done by the coworkers during government work hours. Everyone that attends the 2-3 hour retirement party is on government time using government facilities.

If you were to ask management about this, their reply would simply be that all of these employees are using personal time-off, generally referred to as "leave" and that they are not on government time. This is of course not the case.

This would not be a big deal if there were only a few retirements every year; but nearly a week goes by without seeing a posting for someone's retirement party.

While we are on the subject of parties we can't ignore the many other events that occur every year within every government agency. Family days is an annual event that typically last for half the work day. Many employees have their children and spouses in attendance.

There are also various multicultural days at each agency which is very similar to family days; although with an ethnic theme. Black, Asian, Latin and even LGBT days fall into this category of celebrations. You guessed it, these events are all held during work hours and most attending employees are on government time.

Stupid Spending

The government is extremely reckless when it comes to spending our tax dollars. We've all heard how much the government pays for a hammer; $100 for a plain old hammer when private industry pays about $3 for the same hammer. Just Google "$100 government hammer" and see for yourself.

Now, can you just imagine what the government pays for really expensive items like computers? Our federal law enforcement agencies are as bad as every other agency in this area. It really doesn't need to be this bad and in the solutions section I will address how we can solve all stupid spending in our newly formed combined agency.

So, let's take a look at some areas of current stupid spending.

Computers and Software

The government spends more money for computers and software than they spend for any another expenditure category. Law enforcement makes use of computers and software as much if not more so than most other agencies. A single software product can cost in excess of one billion dollars and there are scores of software components that have cost the government in excess of several million dollars each.

On the surface, this actually doesn't even sound possible.

Let's take a look at just one software product for example. Do you remember the rollout of HealthCare.gov? That's the website that was developed by the government in support of Obama Care. If you recall, it actually didn't work for many months after the rollout causing many people and businesses a lot of online pain and suffering. That simple web site cost the tax payers more than one billion dollars to develop.

A billion dollars for a website??? Ask any large private industry company how much it would have cost them to have developed this website for the government. You can be certain that private industry would have saved the government hundreds and hundreds of millions of dollars. And the website would have actually worked on day one.

Actually, during that debacle some private companies offered to assist the government in this effort. They were told that the government could handle it on their own. The truth is that they didn't want responsible outsiders to see the train wreck that was taking place internally.

While HealthCare.gov has nothing to do with law enforcement agencies, there are countless examples most of which are secret or classified where these agencies have similar computer and software expenditure obscenities.

So, why is this and why do we allow this to continue?

Surprisingly, the reason is very simple. Beltway bandits and the lack of private industry oversight. The vast majority of software and computers are procured or developed by outside companies; collectively, these companies are called the Beltway Bandits, and for good reason.

Since private industry is not involved or tasked with auditing government transactions of this nature, all deals happen behind closed doors out of sight from the people that foot the bill, the tax payer.

See the "Beltway Bandits" section in this book to better understand who they are and why they exist.

Window Washing

Let's turn our attention away from a massive expense item to one that is at the other end of the spectrum. Although not as much as you might think. Every government agency has hundreds or even thousands of buildings located nationwide. Have you witnessed window washers in the middle of winter at a government building and thought that's weird.

Again, it comes down to stupid spending on the government's behalf. It's not just window cleaning, keep in mind that these thousands of government buildings need to have many standard types of services performed on a routine basis. You can be sure that if outside auditors were to compare what the government pays for these services as compared to what private industry pays we would discover extreme stupid spending well into the billions of dollars.

If government agencies were required to publish a monthly report that is disseminated to the general public, that documented all expenditures by location, this type of stupid spending would quickly come to an end. Here's an example of what a report of this nature could look like for our newly formed agency:

Property Expenses for the Month of June 2017				
	Landscaping		**Window_Cleaning**	
	June	**YTD**	**June**	**YTD**
Albany	12,500	65,000	150	400
Buffalo	7,400	7,900	300	600
Dayton	8,700	11,200	1,800	4,200
Tampa	35,600	76,300	350	750
. . .				

This sample report only shows four office locations and two expense items, but it illustrates our point.

Simple reporting would make our government agencies accountable for all of their expenditures. A report of this nature would allow concerned tax payers to question outrageous spending habits.

As shown in this sample report, one would question why Albany and Tampa spend so much more than the other locations on landscaping services. They would also question why Dayton needs to spend $4,200 for window cleaning as compared to much smaller amounts spent by the other cities.

Tax payers should be provided this type of reporting on a monthly basis as a standard practice.

Printers and Ink

Let's take a look at another area where all government agencies especially federal law enforcement agencies spend our tax dollars in an extremely reckless manner. Printers and printer ink is just one of many examples of extreme and unnecessary exorbitant spending.

Spend a few hours in any government building and you'll notice that almost every office you pass has a printer in it, which is normally sitting idle. These printers are not the type of printers we have in our homes or even in many businesses. These printers are high speed, full sized multifunction color printers. Generally referred to as MFP's or multi-function printers. They have print, copy, fax and email functions; maybe they can even make you a cup of coffee. :)

Wonder how much the government pays for the average MFP? Well, that's only part of the problem. Why are there so many and why do they need to be color?

As we know from our own personal experiences, when we go to an office supply store to buy a color cartridge for our inexpensive desktop ink jet printers, we can easily expect to pay more than $50 for a single color cartridge. You can be sure the government is paying hundreds and possibly over a thousand dollars for a single ink cartridge for their MFP's.

There are few reasons why the government should need to print in color.

Black ink printers would do the job just as well. While the reports would not be as pretty; but for internal documents, who really cares.

I can tell you that the printer supply companies care big time. This is a billion dollar government expenditure that is totally out of control. Again, this comes down to a total and complete disregard for the tax payers' money.

Private industry figured out real fast that they need to have shared printers for each floor within an office building; so, instead of having 40 printers on each floor they have a print-room that may have 6 or 8 shared printers.

It would not be surprising to learn that federal law enforcement agencies could very easily save billions every year on printers alone. Instead that money should be better spent finding and arresting bad guys and terrorist.

Office Labor Pool

Government agencies hire college graduates to perform routine office support activities while private industry uses lower waged employees for these functions. Within the government they have a fancy title, typically called OST's or office service technicians.

The functions performed by OST's include mail delivery services, office setup, conference room setup, furniture movement and the such. They are also typically responsible for stocking office supplies and break room supplies.

An OST will typically start at a salary of 40k; add to this approximately 25k for the average cost of employee benefits bringing the total annual cost to 65k for an OST.

Private industry's average cost for the same job function is approximately 30k which includes benefits.

Nationally, there are thousands of OST's; the net result is another gigantic annual expenditure and another way our government misuses our tax payer dollars.

I could go on and on identifying many more areas of stupid spending; although, I would imagine that you get the point and would like to understand how this mess can be fixed.

Although before I get to that, I do need to address one of the largest problems that all agencies have, especially our law enforcement agencies. That's the subject of the Beltway Bandits.

Beltway Bandits

Let's investigate the Beltway Bandits. To do so let's first refer to the definition of "Beltway Bandits" found in Wikipedia:

Beltway bandit is a term for private companies located in or near Washington, D.C. whose major business is to provide consulting services to the US government. The phrase was originally a mild insult, implying that the companies preyed like bandits on the largesse of the federal government, but it has lost much of its pejorative nature and is now often used as a neutral, descriptive term.

The name comes from the Capital Beltway, the ring road that surrounds

Washington. (The entire road is officially called Interstate 495, although the eastern half is cosigned with Interstate 95, which traverses most of the East Coast.) The majority of private contractors are located, or at least headquartered, at intersections along this road in order to be close to federal agencies and legislators. There is a tendency for contractors for the various civilian departments and agencies to locate along the Maryland portion of the Beltway, while defense contractors locate nearer to the Pentagon, along the Virginia section.

The following is a list of just a few of the very large companies that are generally known as Beltway Bandit companies:

(companies listed alphabetically)

- BAE Systems
- Boeing
- Booz Allen Hamilton
- CACI
- CSC
- Deloitte
- DynCorp
- General Dynamics
- General Electric
- IBM
- Lockheed Martin
- ManTech
- Northrup Grumman
- SAIC
- SSI Services
- USIS

Most of the companies listed above are recognizable names because they are massive corporations that have operated in the D.C. beltway for many years. There are literally many hundreds of other companies that are also large beltway bandit companies.

All of these companies share one common goal; generate as much revenue as possible via government contracts.

Most of the beltway bandit companies are very successful, and generate billions of dollars in revenue; some of which have generated trillions of dollars in revenue over recent years.

These companies thrive on the fact that most government agencies, as mentioned earlier, have shameful work ethics and they consistently spend stupid in a very large way. This provides the perfect playing field for the beltway bandits.

When a government agency needs to acquire outside services, they generate an RFP or request for proposal. A process that allows any pre-approved company to reply or bid on that specific RFP. This is a process that can take months with many back and forth communications between the two parties. Eventually, a contract company is selected and a contract is awarded.

Many RFP's are massive in scope and require many resources for extended periods of time. Government agencies have come to rely on outside companies to provide the vast majority of services for all agencies.

The beltway bandits know that the agencies don't have the resources to get the job done on their own and to be honest these government agencies really want to pass the buck to outside companies rather than using internals resources. It's simply the course of least resistance; it's common practice and is the expected solution.

There is a completely different paradox that exists for private industry. For example, when a company like Amazon needs some new software developed, they do it in-house with their own employees. If necessary they hire additional employees as required for specific projects. They control the entire process from the beginning to the end. They are not subject to the outrageous cost associated with using beltway bandit companies.

In order to understand the level of stupidity involved we need to look at a small example where an agency has a small contract requirement. Let's say it's a task that will take one computer programmer exactly one year to complete. Let's say that the skills required of this computer programmer results in that person having a market value of earning an annual salary of $100,000. If the government were to hire a new government employee and task them with this project they would end up incurring somewhere around $140,000 in expenses. This factors in the cost of their benefits plan by adding $40k to their base salary.

Although, since stupid is as stupid does, the government generates an RFP for the task. They go through the RFP selection process and award an annual contract of $485k. In turn, the contract company hires a suitable programmer for maybe $120k, factors in another $40k in benefits for a total cost of

$165k and they realize a wonderful profit of approximately $220K.

What a deal, right?

Now, just imagine how the numbers add up when they are dealing with contracts that have hundreds or even thousands of contractors, for projects that last for many years in duration.

This explains why so many of the top level executives and marketing people in the beltway bandit companies quickly become very rich.

They thank the tax payers all the way to the bank for allowing our government agencies to give away our hard earned tax dollars.

Have you ever had the pleasure of driving around the actual D.C. beltway? It's actually called Interstate 495 and it's approximately 60 miles in length. Try counting the total number of high rise office complexes you pass during a trip around the beltway. You would be counting office complexes that are for the most part owned and operated by the beltway bandit companies.

On second thought, don't try to count them; you'll just get dizzy and nauseous in the process. Although if you want to know where a very large portion of your tax dollars go, you don't need to look any further.

The beltway bandit companies are engaged with every federal law enforcement agency and in fact they are engaged with every government agency; period. When President Trump talks about draining the swamp you can be certain that the swamp creatures are mostly beltway bandits.

Everything Cyber

What exactly is cyber? Cyber is typically used as a prefix to identify one of many internet or computer related crimes. Some of the more common cybercrimes we hear about are cyber-terrorism, cyber-warfare, cyber-sex and cyber-bulling.

All of the federal law enforcement agencies have dedicated a large number of resources to combating cyber-crimes.

The problem that we face is that the bad guys and terrorist always seems to be more advanced and several steps ahead of the good guys when it comes to exploiting all things cyber.

Combining the cyber forces of the various intelligence agencies into a single cyber unit will be a big step in the right direction of combating cyber-crimes. Although this is truly an uphill battle and the good guys need some help to get an edge-up on the bad guys.

Hackers are constantly targeting key software products looking for tiny cracks that can be exploited for nefarious reasons. Highly popular software products such as the Windows operating system and many key software products that run on windows are notorious for being hacked.

Hackers are very smart computer programmers that spend many hours looking for vulnerabilities in all software products, especially those that are directly related to the internet or to social media components.

Unfortunately, the software companies are actually part of the problem. The opportunities for hackers are created by the software companies as a result of their products not taking the necessary precautions to shield against future nefarious usage.

Software products should have a process embedded within, that could significantly reduce viruses and malware from propagating through the internet.

If timely security patches were to take place many software viruses would be unable to spread from one system to another. If software companies would have simply incorporated this into their base design via automatic updates we would have far fewer problems than we have today. This could easily take place automatically on a daily basis as each user connects to the internet. Unfortunately, software vendors rely on users to perform security updates at their leisure and we know the results of that approach.

For years, the Microsoft Corporation made billions of dollars and didn't even provide antivirus protections within the core of the windows operating system. They choose to leave this task to 3rd party software companies. The 3rd party software companies were always behind the eight ball and playing catch-up as new versions of windows were released. In addition, the antivirus products that were available were software add-ons that came with a hefty annual fee. This resulted in many users electing to go without any antivirus protection software for their systems.

The real problem is that antivirus software components cannot be an afterthought or come as a result of add-ons. The protection must be cooked-in to the base software component during the design and development of the software.

Unfortunately, most software companies are more concerned with profitability than they are about delivering software that can't be hacked.

Microsoft is not the only software company at fault in this area. Most of the other large software companies share the blame. Companies such as Apple, Facebook, Twitter and many other social app companies are just as guilty as Microsoft.

Cyber-bullying is another category of cyber that is truly unfortunate. Many young people have committed suicide as a result of being bullied using social media. Again, the fault lies with the software companies that have developed and support their social media products. The largest of which is Facebook.

We must understand that young people today use social media as a way of life. Right or wrong, many adolescents are addicted to social media and when other immature peers attack them using social media it can be devastating. The attacks are not an in-person one-on-one style attack; rather it's a public attack that invites other immature peers to gang-on.

Cyber-bullying can easily be stopped; but only by the social media software companies themselves. They must spend more money and resources on monitoring all communications that takes place using their software products. Again, at this point they care more about their profitability than they do about protecting our young people from cyber-bulling.

Not as a small aside but this is the same issue that has allowed terrorist to recruit American citizens to join their brutal organizations of terror. They have done this in plain sight using social media knowing full well that the software companies were just simply not paying attention.

Since the software industry is completely unregulated, they have no legal responsibilities, they basically can do whatever they want to do with regard to these types of issues. Unfortunately, they can actually create software programs that are specifically designed to help people communicate with one another and remain completely anonymously.

Cyber-terrorism comes in many forms. One such form is also called ransom-ware. This occurs when computer hackers gain access to computer system and essentially disable access to the entire system. In many cases the locked computer displays a message and demands a ransom be paid prior to having the system unlocked.

Ransom-ware is basically a virus that can spread quickly within a business, disabling every computer within the organization. This has happen many times to hospital systems essentially shutting down the entire medical center until a ransom is paid.

This brings us to the subject of **cyber-currency**. Basically, cyber-currency is also known as digital-currency. It can be defined as an internet-based form of currency or medium of exchange distinct from physical (such as banknotes and coins) that exhibits properties similar to physical currencies, but allows for instantaneous transactions and borderless transfer-of-ownership.

Today, the most popular cyber-currency is a product called Bitcoin. The problem that exists with cyber-currencies is that transactions can't be traced. In other words, if someone pays you in bitcoins there is no way for anyone including law enforcement agencies to discover the parties involved in the transaction. It's pretty much like accepting a bag of cash in a dark alley late at night.

The real problem with cyber-currencies is that bad guys figured out real fast that they can very easily use it as ransom for any crime they commit. Thousands of computers have been infected with a virus that basically holds their computer data for ransom until the infected user pays a ransom fee via bitcoin.

Crimes don't even need to be cyber-crimes for criminals to use bitcoin as their method of payment. It could be used as payment for drug deals, kidnapping, child trafficking and many other illegal transactions.

Cyber-currencies are very frequently used as payment for illegal products and services.

There is also something called the "dark web", also known as the "deep web". It's an area that is expressly used for nefarious reasons. Specially designed software products are needed to gain access to this area of the internet. Law abiding citizens don't use or even have knowledge of how to access the "dark web", although criminals make use of the "dark web" on a regular basis to communicate with other criminals. It's their social media underground.

The bottom line is that there are many areas of cyber-terror which our law enforcement agencies need to focus upon. This is an area that will continue to rapidly expand in the coming years. This is one of the major reasons why we will be much better equipped by having a single federal law enforcement agency that can put forth maximum and consolidated resources to get ahead of all cyber related crimes.

Our current federal law enforcement agencies in conjunction with congress must do a much better job at cracking down on all forms of illegal cyber activities. Keep in mind that we are still in the very early days of cyber; just imagine how much worse this can get if we allow this to continue.

Drug Overdoses

How many people need to overdose on a daily basis before we get really serious about this national epidemic? Every year now more than 60,000 people die from overdosing. The number has sky rocketed over the recent years. In 2010 the number was under 40,000 per year. Why is this? Why can't this be stopped?

So many people from all walks of life, all age groups, all ethnicities. In the time it took for you to read the last few sentences, it's likely that several more people have just overdosed.

The drugs that are on the market today are so powerful that for some it just takes one dose to become addicted. The only way to curb this problem is to stop the flow of illegal drugs into our country.

We have depended on federal law enforcement agencies like the ATF and the Customs and Border Protection with fixing this problem. Well, the evidence is in; they are failing with a score of -60,000.

They do the best that they can but they simply don't have enough man-power to be effective.

We need a better solution and we need it right now.

If our federal law enforcement agencies stop spending stupid as addressed in this book we would have plenty of additional funds to put towards stopping the flow of illegal drugs that pour across our borders everyday.

This is not rocket science; we simply need more resources assigned to the task of border protection and we really do need a wall on our southern border. The only solution is to drastically cut down on the flow of illegal drugs that make it across the border everyday.

The profit involved with moving illegal drugs across the border is massive. With a porous border these drugs will continue to flow into our country and will only increase as time goes on.

The organized crime syndicates that exist in Mexico and other countries are ruthless and will do whatever it takes to get their drugs into the U.S. This problem will grow exponentially until we are successful in closing off the border.

Let's not wait until the levels of overdoses exceed 100,000 every year before we solve this devastating problem.

Identity Theft

Another problem that faces our federal law enforcement agencies is identity theft. In most cases, criminals steal someone's social security number and are able to open accounts using their identity.

Every federal law enforcement agency has resources assigned to fighting this problem. A combined agency will be better equipped to deal with these issues from a national perspective.

As law abiding citizens we must understand that identity theft impacts all of us even if we personally have never been a victim of identity theft. It's the merchants and the credit card companies that normally foot the bill for the vast majority of financial losses.

The victim is certainly impacted in a negative manner; although, typically they are free of any fraudulent charges that landed on their accounts.

The credit card companies and merchants absorb the losses; although truth be told, they simply pass these costs back to the consumer in the way of higher credit card interest rates or for merchants by simply increasing the price of all of their products.

So, don't ever lose sight of who actually pays for these losses. You do.

It is estimated that in the U.S. alone, identity theft accounts for approximately three billion dollars annually.

There are ways to stop identity theft. One of such method is called two-factor authentication (TFA). If an opt-in TFA existed for all credit charge transactions were implemented it would have a profound effect on identifying credit card transactions that are attempted using a stolen card. Basically, the way this works is anytime your credit card is used you would receive a text message on your cell phone. You would simply tap either "allow" or "fraud" buttons to complete the transaction.

Both brick and mortar store charges or charges via the internet would work well in a TFA environment. For example, let's say you are at your local grocery store and use one of your credit cards to pay for your groceries. Immediately after you swipe your credit card you would receive a text message that will allow you to confirm this transaction.

Then, if your credit card or credit card number is stolen, the same process happens. You get a text message at the time of the transaction and you would obviously tap on the fraud link since you know that it's not you making the purchase. The criminal that is attempting to use your credit card would be unsuccessful and immediately the cashier would receive a message indicating that this person is very likely to be using a stolen credit card.

Works extremely well; we simply need our federal law enforcement agencies working with congress to pass legislation that requires the implementation of TFA for all credit card transactions in the country.

As a devil's advocate one may say, that's fine but not everyone has the ability to text. This is true and in reality those people often pay with cash and don't have credit cards either. Also keep in mind that there could be alternate methods of payments designed to allow this to work for people that don't have text abilities.

Always remember who pays for identity theft, you do. TFA offers a simple solution; we just need the feds to make this happen.

Election Tampering

Election tampering and voter fraud has long been topics of conversation in our country. It is imperative that federal law enforcement agencies improve the safety and reliability of our election systems and put safe guards in place to ensure that voter fraud is never an issue.

It's clear that the feds are not doing everything that needs to be done in these areas.

Everyone is well aware that voter fraud comes into play every election. We deserve a more full proof system to ensure that voter fraud never impacts the outcome of any election, local, state or federal.

We expect that federal law enforcement agencies will work diligently to eliminate any voter fraud possibilities from future elections.

We understand that election systems are maintained at local and state levels; but since this is a national problem with significant possible consequences we must rely upon federal law enforcement agencies to ensure that these systems are guarded in an effective manner.

In recent years, we are well aware that foreign governments have attempted to tamper with these systems using cyber methods. Federal law enforcement agencies are tasked with ensuring that foreign operatives do not succeed in impacting our election systems.

Once again, a combined federal law enforcement agency will be better equipped to deal with these issues.

Agency Missions

As previously stated, I believe that the 15 primary federal law enforcement agencies need to be combined. The most effective way to accomplish this would be to bring together a select group of law enforcement leaders. This group would be tasked with laying the groundwork and designing the most effective structure for a new consolidated federal law enforcement agency.

The objective would be to focus on building a new agency that is lean although extremely functional in fighting terrorism and protecting our country from all major crime.

Once the framework is designed, the new agency will begin to take shape by acquiring manpower and resources from each of the current agencies in addition to acquiring resources from private industry.

An aggressive three year plan should be developed to complete the build-out of the new agency, with the understanding that the 15 individual agencies would be shut down at the end of this three year period.

As one can imagine, there will be many people that will totally disagree with the idea of merging these agencies. Some will say that each of these agencies have different missions and combining these agencies simply does not make sense.

As previously stated, the number one goal of each of these agencies is to protect us from the bad guys. Additionally there are a few agencies that seem to have a more targeted mission then others, the ATF and Secret Service are two examples of agencies that have very specific missions.

It is important to understand that there are dozens of very specific examples that require the focus of our federal law enforcement resources; however, that does not mean that we need separate agencies to combat each of these specific areas. If that were the case, we would have individual agencies for child pornography, identity theft, cyber, bank robberies, white-collar crime and many others.

There is no reason why a single agency can't be tasked to address all of these areas and do so in a more efficient and effective manner. There is simply far too much overhead and bloat associated with each individual government agency.

We will need to be prepared and expect significant resistance from within each of the agencies. The leadership within each agency will be very much opposed to a merger of this nature. They will instinctively feel obligated to "protect their empire". Their number one goal is to protect their turf, period.

Resistance will also come from many outside entities. The beltway bandits will be first in line. They will be up in arms over this idea and will attempt to influence Congress to come to their defense. Fortunately, there are more of us than there are of them, so let's make sure that Congress remembers who they actually work for.

Solutions

As one can imagine, the solution to all of these issues is complicated. Although that does not mean that it can't be accomplished. The best way to take on any large problem is to simply take one step at a time and not worry about the big picture. Keep this in mind as you read the steps as outlined below.

1. First and foremost, we need congress to do their job!

   We must impress upon them that this is a matter of extreme importance. Time is of the essence and that we require congress to move quickly on addressing these issues.

So please, notify your local and state representatives in congress that you want the following federal law enforcement agencies to be merged into a single agency (tell them to read "messed up" for all of the details):

- ATF - Bureau of Alcohol, Tobacco, Firearms
- CIA - Central Intelligence Agency
- DCIS - Defense Criminal Investigative Service
- DEA - Drug Enforcement Administration
- DHS - Department of Homeland Security
- DIA - Defense Intelligence Agency
- FBI - Federal Bureau of Investigation

- ICE - Immigration and Customs Enforcement
- NCIS - Naval Criminal Investigative Services
- NSA - National Security Agency
- USCBP - United States Customs and Border Protection
- USCP - United States Capitol Police
- USMS - United States Marshals Service
- USPIS - United States Postal Inspection Service
- USSS - United States Secret Service

2. Inform your friends to do the same. We need large numbers to get the attention of congress. If you use social media please share your recommendation with your network of contacts.

3. Let's impress upon congress that the need to solve these issues is extremely important and demand that they move forward on this issue now; not later. It is a matter of urgency.

4. The newly formed agency needs to begin with a totally different culture than currently exists within today's government agencies. Many of the following items will require a complete 180 in the way government agencies function and are structured. We need a totally new culture in every way possible. This new agency can and should be an example for agency mergers in other areas of the federal government.

5. The newly formed federal law enforcement agency must be mandated to use a 60/40 rule. In that 60 percent of

all employees within the new agency must be either agents or intelligence analysts. Support staff and management staff should never exceed 40 percent of the total work force. Let's require more boots on the ground to make sure that we continually focus on stopping the bad guy and terrorist before they impact additional innocent citizens.

6. Employees of the new agency should be outside of the current government pay structure and its limitations. No standard government GS pay levels should exist within the new agency. Employees should be hired in a fashion more akin to how private industry hires its work force. Every employee is to be paid a negotiated salary during the hiring process. Employees should receive an annual salary increase and bonuses entirely

based on individual employee performances; exactly the way private industry functions.

7. This newly formed agency must not use more than 20 percent of its total allocated budget for outside contract services. This basically results in the agency needing to hire full-time employees of the agency to perform the vast majority of required tasks. The end result is that this new agency will not be dependent on and at the mercy of the Beltway Bandits any longer.

8. Employees of the new agency should be provided incentives to reduce the cost and deliver projects ahead of schedule. Similar to the way that private industry incentives their work force. Currently, agencies attempt to generate employee

commitment and esprit de corps by pushing the do-it for your country idea. The reality is that this seldom actually works.

9. Petition congress to move forward on regulating the entire software industry. The only way to stop cyber-crime at all levels is from within the software that runs our computers and smartphone devices. The software companies will never do this on their own. We must insist that congress moves forward on passing legislation that requires the regulation and government oversight within the software industry. We have government regulations for light bulbs, for automobiles, for suntan lotion and every other item under the sun, except for software. And in this day and age, software can do us more harm than

almost any other product. This needs to change and it needs to change very quickly. It is my intent to write a separate book on the subject of "Regulate The Software Industry" in the coming months.

10.   Petition congress to stop the flow of illegal drugs into our country. Congress needs to dictate that the new federal law enforcement agency increases their efforts and resources in stopping the flow of illegal drugs, especially via our southern border.

11.   Petition congress to pass legislation that requires all cyber currency transactions to identify each participant engaged in a transaction to be fully identifiable. This will eliminate the possibility of criminals holding private citizens and companies hostage and

requiring payment via a cyber-currency such as Bitcoin.

12.   Require that the new agency does not make the mistake of playing musical chairs with its work force. Require that employees do what they are hired to do and what they are trained to do. Federal agents are trained to be skilled law enforcement officers; they should not perform duties beyond this capacity. Too often in the current federal law enforcement agencies you will find that trained agents are placed into admin like departments such as human resources or in I.T. departments.

13.   As the new federal agency begins to take shape, each of the current agencies should be downsized over a

period not to exceed three years where they can be completely shuttered.

14.   Insist that the new agency is required to actively engage with private industry. Representatives from private companies should be tasked on a quarterly basis to review and evaluate all agency expenditures. Their findings should be documented and made available to the public. This will put an end to reckless spending that has gone on far too long in our government agencies.

15.   Engage in open and civil dialog on the subject of reestablishing the power of the FCC. Quite possibly the time has come where we need to return to a level of civility when communicating using any public conduit, i.e. via cable TV,

broadcast TV, apps or the internet. We have become very aware that political discourse so often reverts to extreme measures for some individuals including reverting to violence.

As you can see, many of the actions require initiatives taken by congress. But always remember that congress answers to you, the voter. You only need to be persistent to make sure that they listen to the people that put them in office and allow them to stay in office.

Impossible

Some will say that it's simply not possible to merge all of these agencies together.

I will argue that "Anything Is Possible". Case in point is the Department of Homeland Security. This agency didn't even exist prior to 9/11. And now that agency is one of the largest agencies in the federal government.

The problem with DHS is that it's just another typical government agency, patterned after all of the others.

Let's never make that mistake again. As stated in the book, we need to pattern our agencies along the lines of private industry in every way possible.

And yes, we will need the support of congress which won't be easy. We are quite aware that congress always seems to be paralyzed with so many patrician issues.

In order for this objective to be achieved, it needs to be supported by both the right and the left of the political spectrum. Fortunately, both sides of the isle do realize that government agencies are extremely dysfunctional and hopefully they will agree that now is the time to undertake the re-design of how our government agencies are structured and function.

Everyone knows that our government is broken in so many ways; the hope is that we can conclude that now is the time to start anew and there is no better place to start than with our federal law enforcement agencies.

You Name It

You may have noticed that at no point in the book have I suggested what the name of the new federal law enforcement agency should be.

This is a task that I believe should be decided upon by the general public.

Do you have a suggestion for an appropriate name for this new federal law enforcement agency?

If you have what you think would be a suitable name please email this name to the following email address: messedupgov@gmail.com

If this book becomes a best seller we are certain to find the very best and most appropriate name for this new agency.

Your Call to Action

As stated, there are approximately 2 million people working for our federal law enforcement agencies with a combined annual budget of more than 2 trillion dollars. Since these agencies are not forthcoming in a timely manner in publishing their actual numbers, my numbers are estimated using the most recently available data and could be off by 20 percent in one direction or another.

Regardless, I am 100 percent certain that we are spending far too much and that we are definitely not getting what we pay for.

If you agree that it's time to fix our federal law enforcement agencies, please get involved today and help us make America a better and safer nation. Notify as many people as you can and invite them to join this effort. Most importantly, notify congress as often as you can and recommend that they move forward on these issues.

Thank You!
Jim Kitty

Terror After 9/11

Listed below in chronological order are 16 terror attacks that have occurred in the United States since 9/11. We can only hope that this list does not continue to grow:

March 3, 2006 - Chapel Hill, North Carolina

Mohammed Reza Taheri-azar, a 22-year-old Iranian drove his SUV into a crowd of students at the University of North Carolina. He injured six people. He said that he did this as retribution for the treatment of Muslims around the world.

June 1, 2009 - Little Rock, Arkansas

Abdulhakim Muhammad, opened fire at an army recruitment office, killing one soldier and wounding another. Muhammad was a 23-year-old Muslim convert, a self-radicalized homegrown terrorist. He was motivated for the attack over the wars in Iraq and Afghanistan.

November 5, 2009 - Fort Hood, Texas

Army psychiatrist, Major Hasan, 44-year-old, opened fire at a military processing center at Fort Hood, Texas. He killed 13 people and wounded 32. His apparent motivation was by former Yemeni al-Qaeda leader Anwar al-Awlaki, shouting "Allahu Akbar!" during the attack.

April 15, 2013 - Boston, Massachusetts

Brothers Tamerlan Tsarnaev, 26-year-old, and Dzhokhar Tsarnaev, 19-year-old, detonated two backpacks containing homemade pressure-cooker bombs near the finish line of the Boston Marathon. The bombs detonated 10 seconds apart, killing three people and maiming 17 others.

July 18, 2014 - Washington State & New Jersey

Ali Muhammad Brown shot and killed Leroy Henderson and Dwone Anderson-Young in Washington State. He then drove to New Jersey and shot and killed Brendan Tevlin. Brown admitted to the murders, describing each as a 'just kill.' He declared his adherence to Islam and said that he was angry at the 'evil' occurring in the U.S.

October 23, 2014 - New York City, New York

Zale Thompson, a recent Islam convert to Islam attacked four New York City police officers in broad daylight with a hatchet; slashing one on the arm and hitting another in the head before being shot and killed by another officer. One officer was hit in the head and was critically injured but survived. Thompson frequently posted on social media his support for jihad and guerrilla warfare against the U.S.

July 16, 2015 - Chattanooga, Tennessee

Mohammad Youssef Abdulazeez, shot and killed four Marines and a sailor on Chattanooga military bases. He was inspired and motivated by foreign terrorist organization's propaganda.

November 4, 2015 - Merced, California

Faisal Mohammad stabbed four individuals in the University of California-Merced campus. He was shot and killed by law enforcement afterwards. Mohammad may have been self-radicalized as no evidence of a direct connection with ISIS has been discovered.

December 2, 2015 - San

Bernardino, California

Syed Rizwan Farook and his wife Tashfeen Malik, originally from Pakistan, attacked a disabilities and development center in San Bernardino, killing 14 of Farook's coworkers. The two were later killed by law enforcement following a road-side shootout. Malik had reportedly devoted allegiance to ISIS.

December 31, 2015 - Rochester,

New York

Emanuel Lutchman had reported his allegiance for ISIS online as well as his hatred for America. He attacked a local restaurant/bar in Rochester, New York, with a machete and knives on New Year's Eve.

January 7, 2016 - Philadelphia, Pennsylvania

Edward Archer, 30, shot and wounded a Philadelphia Police Officer. According to the police, Archer had pledged allegiance to ISIS.

June 12, 2016 - Orlando, Florida

Omar Mateen attacked the Pulse nightclub in Orlando with several firearms; killing 49 and injuring more than 50 before police stormed the building and killed Mateen. Mateen talked to a 911 operator and announced his allegiance to ISIS during the attack.

September 17, 2016 - St. Cloud, Minnesota

Dahir Ahmed Adan began stabbing several individuals before an off-duty police officer shot and killed him. According to police,

Adnan asked one person if they were a Muslim before attacking him. The ISIS news organization, Amaq, claimed that Dahir was one of their supporters.

September 17, 2016 - New York and New Jersey

Ahmad Rahami shot and injured two police officers before being shot himself. Earlier that day he had planted and detonated pressure-cooker bombs in Manhattan and in Seaside Park, New Jersey. 31 individuals were injured.

November 28, 2016 - Columbus, Ohio

Abdul Ali Artan drove a car into a crowd of pedestrians at Ohio State University and then attacked them with a knife, injuring 11. A police officer then shot and killed Artan. Artan expressed support for ISIS and al-Qaeda on Facebook just before the attack.

June 21, 2017 - Flint, Michigan

Mor Ftouhi, a Canadian/Tunisian dual citizen, attacked a police officer at Bishop International Airport in Flint. Reports state that he shouted and said "You have killed people in Syria, Iraq, and Afghanistan, and you are all going to die."

Book Review

I would greatly appreciate your review of this book. Regardless of whether you acquired the book in eBook format or if you purchased a hard copy print version of the book.

Authors like myself depend on timely reviews of their books.

Thank you very much.
Jim Kitty

www.ingramcontent.com/pod-product-compliance
Lightning Source LLC
Chambersburg PA
CBHW032113280326
41933CB00009B/820